The Stories Beh

1. **Reflection of My Heart** - When I decided to put together a collection of my poems, my best friend wanted to know what I was going to call it and I decided on Reflection of my Heart because basically that is what the words are. Sometimes the poems have significant meanings to me and sometimes words just come to me, and I write them down, with no real explanation for the poem at all.
So, then she said you need to write a Poem called that, so I did.
2. **Now That I'm gone** - I wrote this for my mom a few days before she passed away. Then they read it at her funeral.
3. **Well Done** -This was written after a very good sermon at Church. My ex- boss had this read at her mother's funeral.
4. **Keep Your Faith** - I wrote this for my Mother-in-Law, she was very ill at the time and her life expectancy was only five years, she kept her faith and she lived way beyond their expectations.
5. **Special Child** - I was having a very bad day at work, when a little girl with Down Syndrome whom I had never seen before came through our store. She saw me and blew me the biggest kiss and smiled the most beautiful smile. Without thinking I immediately blew one back to her just as her mother turned and looked at me. We began talking and I learned her Name was Amy, she was three years old

and talked in sign language. I went back to work and kept thinking about her and forgot all about what my problems were. So, I started writing and within about 5 minutes I had written Special Child. I didn't see them anymore for quite some time then finally one day Amy came into the store with her dad. I told him my story and asked if he would mind taking the poem to his wife for me that I had wrote. He started reading it and began crying. He said I described their feelings perfectly. Since then, we all became good friends, Amy continued talking in sign language but she also began speaking and learned to say my name. And she can also say it in sign language. They gave me a postcard with Amy's picture on it that another Downs Syndrome boy in Indiana drew of her. She truly is a special child.

6. **Thank You!** - The Kids were having a Veterans Day program at School and with many of our Wartime Uncles in mind I wrote it. They read it at the Ceremony, it was the first poem of mine that I had allowed to be read Publicly. There was a good friend of ours, a former FBI Agent that had been suffering from effects of the Gulf War, his son read the poem at the ceremony Him and a few of the other Veterans cried when they heard it. Since then, it has been published in a Paralyzed Veterans of America Magazine, read at several Veterans Day ceremonies, it hangs in the PVA office in Oklahoma City, Oklahoma. The Veterans Administration Office in

Muskogee, Oklahoma. It hangs in the old Proctor school House in Proctor, Oklahoma, it has made it all the way to Iraq and Afghanistan to many Soldiers, but what I am the most Honored and Proud of is that a Former WWII Soldier Oscar J. Nipps A.K.A Jr. thought enough of the Poem to donate it to the Veterans War Memorial Museum in Broken Arrow, Oklahoma were it now hangs beside true Hero Memorabilia.

7. **Heavens' Hope** - was written about a little girl that I heard about on the news one day. She was dying of cancer. Her name was Heaven.
8. **The Orphans Prayer** - Just words that came to me.
9. **Say a Prayer for Mama** - Really worried about my mom when she was having repeated Heart Attacks
10. **The Light** - This was also written with my Mother-in-Law in mind while she was going through more health problems.
11. **A Stones Throw Away** – very good sermon at Church.
12. **My Secret** - This was written for my brother after my mom had passed away, he was having a very hard time dealing with it.
13. **Grandpa's Home** - I was thinking about Grandpa one day and how he used to set me on his knee and rock me in his big old rocking chair while I played with his pocket watch. I was very young when he passed away and that's all I really remember about him.

14. **For My Children** - This one explains itself
15. **The Crossroads of Oklahoma** - There are so many crosses up and down these roads, I had never noticed them in any of the other states I had been in.
16. **Won't it Be Something**- Just thinking about what it must be like arriving in Heaven.
17. **Consider-** Good Preaching
18. **Stepping Stones** – Good Preaching, realizing that the journey we take in life is just stepping stones to where we will eventually be.
19. **Faith** – Just a little pep talk with myself one day.
20. **This Morning**- A very vivid and scary dream
21. **My One true friend** – Just missing my mom.
22. **Surrendered**- More thoughts and words that came to me.
23. **Shelter us**- This was written in the aftermath of 9/11.
24. **He Can Move Your Mountains**-Written after a very good Sermon in church.
25. **Thank You** – Just feeling Thankful and counting my Blessings.
26. **He's the Son** – Just another Pep talk with myself.
27. **Thankful**- Good Preaching
28. **Love Him** – encouraging words to myself again.
29. **I want to see Jesus** – After a good Sermon in Church.

30. **Why Won't They Believe** – Just curious how anyone could not Believe.
31. **Can They See Jesus** – The message in church was about how people can tell if you are a true Christian or not.
32. **Rock for Ages** – Just leaning on the Lord.
33. **Angel in Disguise** – This was written about a good friend who always let the Lord's light shine through her.
34. **Keep on walking** - A friend suggested that I write something about the devil stalking you, so I did.
35. **The Father and The Son** – A good Sermon in church
36. **I'll be Satisfied**-Just a good Sermon in Church
37. **Jesus Hold My Hand** – Just needing a little strength from the Lord that day.
38. **I Believe** - explains itself.
39. **Your Little Boy's Hero** - who knows, it just popped into my head.
40. **40 Years** was written for my Boss on his 40th year in the business, he loved it, and came in to Thank Me personally. He said he had a box in his office where he kept Special things that mean a lot to him, and he said he would put it there, that he really appreciated it. Sadly enough, he passed away a couple of years later.
41. **All Around Cowboy** - A friend wanted one written about her cowboy boyfriend, so I asked her to describe him to me, and this is what I came up with.
42. **Letter from Dad** - Explains itself.

43. **Why did he have to go** - a friend's brother was killed, and she wanted something written for him.
44. **Good Intentions** - Just thoughts that came to me.
45. **Daddy Don't Shout**- Story of my life.
46. **United We Stand-** Just thinking about the problems in this crazy world we live in.
47. **Grandpa-** Missing Grandpa
48. **Remember –** Just a little pep talk.
49. **Through A Childs Eyes** - Just thinking of the innocence and simplicity of a child's thoughts and the way they see life not knowing the struggles of life.
50. **Above and Beyond –** About my dad
51. **The Creature -** About my dad
52. **When My Life is Through –** Just thinking about after I die.
53. **P.O.W –** Paying a tribute to the soldiers again.
54. **A Soldiers Journey –** Just paying Tribute to the Soldiers
55. **Be Still My Heart-** Just thoughts in my head.
56. **Stairway to Heaven-** Just a talk with Grandpa
57. **Window in Heaven –** enjoying a beautiful sunset in Oklahoma that looked like a light shining through a window, and the thought came to me a window in Heaven.

Reflection of My Heart

It's just a reflection of my heart,
I don't know how or when it starts.
It comes from deep within,
There's no beginning or no end.
And I know it is a part,
Of my life, right from the start.
It's all a reflection of my heart.

Sometimes it comes to me in a song,
Or in a poem short or long.
I'll write it down and then go on,
It's a reflection of my heart.

It's just a way that I express,
My deepest hurt or happiness,
And it's when I do my best,
Reflecting of my heart.

Now That I'm Gone

Don't weep for me now that I am gone,
My love will always be with you,
And this will help to make you strong.

My life on earth seemed short I know,
But please don't be sad.
Just remember the memories that we share,
And the good times that we've had.

My life is not over now, it has only just begun.
I did not leave this world alone,
The angels came and took me to Gods' Heavenly throne.

I'm with Jesus now so please don't be sad.
I'm not hurting anymore, no more tears will I shed.
I'll be here waiting for you,
So please don't think of me as dead.

I'm alive and well and I am not alone,
I'm in Heaven with Jesus, At God's Heavenly throne.
So please don't weep for me,
I'm at peace now that I am gone.

Well Done

Each day of my life as I travel on,
I have just one special goal.
To live my life for the Lord that I love so.
And gain the right to walk on streets of gold.

When my life on earth is done,
And I'm standing before the Lord,
He'll look at me and say,
"Well done my child, well done, thank you for believing in me and my Son.
 Though at times it wasn't so easy I know. When the mountains were high and the valleys were low,
And you could have given up, but you didn't let go.
Well done, my child, well done."

Then he'll open the gates and we'll walk on inside,
 With my eyes, full of tears but my heart full of pride,
I'll look up at him, and then I will say,
"Well done my Lord, well done,
Thank you for believing in me through your Son.
Though at times it wasn't so easy I know,
When the mountains were high and the valleys so low,
And I almost gave up, but you didn't let go.
Thank you, my Lord, for loving me so,
Well done my Lord, well done."

Keep Your Faith

Sometimes when life lets you down,
Don't give up.
The walk through the valley,
May seem lonesome and cold.
Just keep your faith,
And one day you'll walk on streets of gold.

You may feel abandoned,
And that you don't have a friend in the world.
But you do have a very special friend,
And you are never alone.

He knows you're hurting it hurts him too,
Just keep your faith and he'll carry you through.
It seems like such a struggle that has no end.

But he'll never give you more than you can bare,
And even though it seems like no one loves you,
Remember God does and he will always care.
So just keep climbing your mountain,
One step at a time.
Keep your faith and one day only glory you will find.

Special Child

Why is their heart so big you say?
Because it's filled with Gods love,
In its own special way.

With a smile, so bright, when they enter a room,
They're sure to delight,
 Full of a love that has no end,
More loving than your very best friend.

They know no stranger yet they are full of fear.
You'll never know how many tears their parents have shed,
Why me they say, why not someone else instead?

If all had the heart of a special child,
all would be full of love, meek and mild.
So, Gods most precious gift,
Is the gift of a Special child.

They teach you to love, have faith and hope,
They lead you to God on the days you can't cope.

So, when you Thank God for his blessings tonight,
Give him a Special Thank you,
For the Special child, he put in your life.

God chose you to lead their way,
Because you are Special too, in your very own way.

Thank You!

This is for the men and women,
Who have fought for a cause.
It's for the ones who made it home,
It's for the ones we lost.

They started out as mere children,
Young boys and young girls.
But in a flash one night,
Things happened,
that would change their world.

Some of them were drafted,
And some went on their own.
But if it weren't for all of them,
We couldn't feel safe at home.

Thanks to the ones who suffered.
Through World War I and World War II
Korea, Vietnam, Desert Storm
and Iraq to name a few.

Thanks to the ones who suffer still,
Whose lives will never be the same.

We Thank you for the price you paid,
And we're sorry for your pain.

You are our unsung Heroes,
Though we may not know your name.
Always know we appreciate you.
And your efforts were not in vain.
Whether you were in during war time,
Or during a time of peace.
Thank You!
If it weren't for you,
We would not be free.

Heavens' Hope

Heaven is a little girl,
So precious, she's just like a pearl.
A love so rare, one of a kind,
She may not have much time.

But rest assured, she's gonna be alright.
Because Heaven's got God on her side.
Though we may not understand,
Heaven knows God has a plan.

Jesus has a rocking chair,
This I know because my baby's there.
It breaks our hearts to see her go,
But we'll see her again, this I know.

Life passes so quickly by,
But we must go on, we've just got to try.
We must treasure our memories,
and remember our little girl is free.

Free from pain, free from this world.
And she'll always be our little girl.
Though it breaks our hearts to see her go.

She's gonna be alright I know.
Because Jesus loves the little children,
All the children of the world.

The Orphans Prayer

One day an orphan child prayed,
And to Jesus these words he said.
He said please help me, I'm all alone,
Please help me Jesus I need a home.

My mommy loved me. I know that's true,
But the angels took her,
Now she's with you.
And as for daddy it's hard to say.
When mommy passed on,
Daddy went away.

Please help me Jesus I'm all alone,
Please help me Jesus I need a home.
If you can find me a happy home,
I'll be safe there, no more I'll roam.
If you can't then take me above.
Take me to Heaven where I'll be loved.
Please help me Jesus, I'm all alone,
Please help me Jesus, I need a home.

Please Say a Prayer for Mama

I see you every Sunday, With your bible and your suit.
I know if I have a problem, I can always count on you
So, when you go to church this Sunday,
There's something I need to ask of you.
Please say a Prayer for Mama, I don't want her to go.
Please say a prayer for mama, Because I love her so.

I don't want to be selfish; I don't mean to be rude.
Please say a prayer for mama Because her lives not through.
She's still a young lady, In search of her dreams.
I know she can find them, if you give her more time you'll see.
But if you need my mama, please tell her not to cry.
I'll still love and miss my mama, but angels never die.

When you're up there at the altar and you bow your head to pray
Please pray for the lady, who couldn't be here today.
Please say a prayer for mama, she deserves more than a few kind words.

I said a prayer for Grandpa, And I know God must have heard.
Please say a prayer for mama I don't want her to go,
Please say a prayer for mama, Because I love her so.

The Light

There's a light each day I wait to see,
And though I feel so lonely,
I know the Lord is with me.

The road is long and sometimes hard,
But one day we'll reach our destination.
There's a Light each day I wait to see.

With pain, as big as a mountain,
And faith as small as a grain of mustard seed.
That light shines a little bit brighter,
The more that I believe.

And one day at the end of the tunnel,
That light is going to shine for me.
So, each day I'll just remember,
Why there's only one set of footprints that I see.

Though it's been a long and painful,
Each step of the way the Lord has carried me.
No one knows how hard our journey is,
Just my Lord and me.
But together we will make it through the tunnel,
We must it's our destiny.

A Stones Throw Away

Each day of your life,
There's something you should do.
Love your brother as you would have him Love you.
Though at times it may seem hard.
Before you cast the first stone,

Look in your own backyard.

Try to walk in the likeness of Jesus,

every day.
Don't let Heaven be a Stone's throw away.
Sometimes you may stumble,
Just don't let yourself fall.

Be a good neighbor,
Be a good friend.
Kindness has no boundaries,
Love has no end.

Before you judge someone else's life,
You should stop and judge your own.
You might not have the chance tomorrow,
To change your ways.
So, don't let Heaven,
Be a stone's throw away.

My Secret

If I had the strength to move a mountain,
I would move it for you.
If I could reach the stars,
I'd use them to light your way.

The only thing I can offer you,
Is the secret to your success,
The answer to your happiness.
The way to relieve your stress.

It's the secret that can move your mountains,
And reach the stars to light your way.
It's the secret that I use in life,
The one that guides me every day.

All you should do is ask for it,
Then believe it will come true.
It works for me each day,
I know it will work for you.
My secret is………God!

Grandpa's Home

Walk with me Jesus so I'm not alone,
Walk right beside me on my journey home.
Shape me and guide me in the way I should be.
Walk with me Jesus as I walk with thee.

When I was just a little one on my grandpa's knee,
He told me of Jesus and how he'd set me free.
He said when you grow up and go out on your own,
Walk close to Jesus, he won't steer you wrong.

He said the road might seem rocky,
And the journey so long.
Child hold on to Jesus and he'll lead you home.

It's been many years since my grandpa's been gone,
He had quite a journey, but he wasn't alone.
And as a small child I remember the day,
The Angels and Jesus took my grandpa away.

I'll always remember what he taught me,
He taught me about Jesus and how he would save me.
Even though I still miss him I am not alone.
I'm walking with Jesus and waiting to see Grandpa,
In Heaven, he's home.

For My Children

I was touched by an angel,
Whenever I had you.
A special gift from up above,
My precious child, it's you.

You gave my life new meaning,
And filled my heart with Love.
God has truly blessed me,
With this gift from above.

You fill my heart with laughter,
With the little things you do.
My little ray of sunshine,
You make my days so bright.

You are my special gift of love,
My every dream come true.
My love is unconditional,
No matter what you do.
And all the blessings in my life,
I will always treasure you.

The Crossroads of Oklahoma

I've traveled across this land,
And many sights I've seen.
But one thing in particular
Means the most to me.

I've traveled down Route 66, and up old 33,
And no matter where I've been,
I've seen the same familiar scene.
The roads are lined with crosses,
Sometimes just one or two.
But far too often they are lined in groups of three.

Each cross has a name on it,
To remind us of someone who used to be.
A loved one lost,
Who remains alive in someone's memory.

Many folks may not realize,
How much these crosses mean to me,
But one thing is for certain,
I've known it from the start.
 The crossroads of Oklahoma,
Will forever cross my Heart.

Won't It Be Something

Won't it be something to wake up in Heaven,
And find out we made it, despite it all.
And to find out our dreaming has finally come true.
Won't it be something to meet with our maker.
The one who created me and you.

We'll listen to stories, By Saints gone before us.
And hear of their struggles, and how they stayed true.
Oh, won't it be something to wake up in Heaven.
And hear how you answered, Gods final call.

We'll walk down the streets, of gold laid before us.
While listening to Angels sing us a tune.
Won't it be something to wake up in Heaven.
And know there is room there, for me and for you.

We'll talk with the Saints and sing with the Angels.
We won't have to worry about life anymore.
We'll meet with our neighbors, and loved ones who,
Have left us.
Oh, what a day that will be.

There'll be singing and shouting and crying and laughter.
And the happiest one there will be me.
Won't it be something, to wake up in Heaven.

And find out I'm there for an eternity.
This morning, I woke up inside Heaven,
And this time it wasn't a dream.

Consider

Sometimes when your burdens, seem more than you can bare.
It seems like life is weighing heavy on you,
And that no one could possibly care. Then it's time to stop and consider,
That you are not alone think about his journey,
And his crown of thorns.

Think of how long his journey must have been,
And how heavy his cross was to him.
Just imagine how his mother,
Through the many tears, she shed
stayed strong,
Even though her only son, soon would be dead.

When you feel it's more, than you can stand.
Consider the journey, the cross, the crown of thorns,
And most of all consider the man.
And when it seems, there's just no hope,
And nowhere left to turn. consider your burdens,
As your own cross that you must bear.

Take your journey one step at a time. stay strong and faithful,
And keep believing, one day I will be there.

And if you have any doubt at all, consider the stone.
Can you just imagine, the pride that Mary felt,
When she realized, Jesus was gone.
You're just a part of Gods great plan, and just as important as anyone.
Because God made you, with his own two hands.
And if you look, you'll find, strength doesn't come from within,
True strength comes from him.

Steppingstones

I'll Thank the Lord above, for my salvation.
And for carrying me along the way. I'll thank him for the
Troubled seas he gave me. for they only made me
stronger,
 every day.

I'll Thank him for the steppingstones, to my salvation.
And I'll keep stepping until, they lead me home one day.
And just when old Satan, thinks he's got me.
I'll just hold tighter to my Jesus, and I know he'll hear me,
When I pray.

Old Satan's just another steppingstone, along life's weary
way.
I'll thank the Lord for my salvation, and the troubled seas,
He calmed along the way; I'll thank him for the life he
gave me.
And for his son, and what he did on Calvary that day.
I'll thank him for the steppingstones, to my salvation.
And for coming back,
To take me home someday.

Faith

Faith is the only thing,
That will pull you through.
When it seems, there is no hope,
You know just what to do.

Get down on your knees,
And Thank the Lord above.
Because you know it would be worse,
If you didn't know his love.

And no matter what the circumstance,
You know he's there.
Give the Lord a fighting chance,
And he will see you through.

The steps you take that seem so long,
Are steps taken by two.
They're just a part of Gods great plan,
He has laid out for you.

Without faith, there is no hope,
And they help to see you through.
So, get down on your knees tonight,
And thank the Lord above.
Give the Lord a fighting chance,
And he'll shelter you with love.

This Morning

When I awoke this morning, I found out I was dead.
Had I died in my sleep, or had I just bumped my head?
Alone in the darkness, afraid, and not knowing which way to go.
With two paths ahead of me, which one should I take?
One of them leading to Heaven, the other assuredly to Hells gates.

I took the one to my left, for it had to be right.
It's the one I had followed all my life.
Slowly I followed this very dark path,
I walked and I walked, with no light in sight.
It seemed like I walked, for three days and three nights.

When suddenly there was a light,
That nearly blinded me. I was not dead, I was awake,
This was a message from God, sent only to me.
He was telling me I needed to choose now.
Which path I would follow, before it is too late.

So, I jumped out of bed and got down on my knees.
I asked for forgiveness of my sins,
And the life I had always chose to lead.
And then I thanked him, for the chance to finally see the light.
And most of all I thanked him, for the change, he had just made in my life.

My One True Friend

You were such a special person,
One true friend indeed.
Always willing to lend a hand,
To anyone in need.

Such a caring way about you,
Like no one else I've known.
It will be hard to live without you,
But life must go on.

Your memories we'll carry with us,
Wherever we may go.
The caring ways you taught us,
We'll share with those we know.

You always gave of yourself,
Whether it be a friendly smile,
Or just a quick Hello.
You always left warm memories,
Wherever you would go,
And rest assured my mother,
Sadly, you will be missed,
More than you will ever know.

Surrendered

I surrender my heart, Lord; I surrender my soul.
Wherever you lead me, that's where I want to go.
Teach me thy ways O Lord, show me thy paths.
Heaven is my future since you forgave me my past.

Lead me in thy truth O Lord, for the rest of my days.
For I know you will be with me, In my heart, every day.
Whatever your plans for me, I won't need to know.
Because wherever you lead me, that's where I want to go.

I'll be climbing the stairway, one step at a time.
But if I should stumble, you'll be right by my side.
I surrender my heart, Lord; I surrender my soul.
Sinning is in the past Lord, now Heaven is my goal.

If the mountain seems high Lord, or the valley is low.
I know you will carry me wherever I go.
I'll meet you in Heaven, some glorious day.
Where I'll continue to Love you, for my eternal days.
I surrendered my heart O Lord; I surrendered my soul.
I gave up my past, to make Heaven my home.

Shelter Us

Lord shelter us with Love,
Bless us all with peace.
Comfort us with strength,
In this our time of grief.

Give us all some hope,
So, that we can see.
Though it seems so hard,
I know if we believe.

Soon there'll be an end,
To this world's tragedies.
So, shelter us with Love,
Bring us to our knees.
Answer this our prayer,
Give the world some peace.

He Can Move Your Mountains

If you have faith,
He can move your mountain.
He knows you're in need,
Just call out his name.
If you're needing strength,
Use him to lean on.
He knows you're hurting,
He feels your pain.

Though you may feel he's left you,
He's the one who is,
Carrying you through.
He's the little voice inside,
Saying you can make it through.
He's helping you through every minute,
Every hour, every day.
He's the one crying with you,
He's the one who's listening,
When you pray.

So, if you have faith,
Ask him to move your mountains.
Hold on tight,
And he'll carry you through.
Believe in him, just as he believes in you.

Thank You

Thank you for the Love You've given me.
And thank you for my friends and family.
Thank you for the strangers, on the street.
And thank you for the ones I've had the chance to meet.

Thank you for your son up above, and thank you for,
His unending love.
Thank you for the birds, that sing so sweet.
And thank you Lord, for each and every thing.
Thank you for your blessings, great and small.
So many now, that I can't count them all.

Even though my life, hasn't always been this way,
I want to thank you Lord, for each day.
Sometimes I don't deserve you, but you love me anyway.

Thank you for the flowers, In the spring.
Thank you, Lord for each and every thing.
Thank you for the shoes upon my feet,
Thank you for the food I have to eat.

Thank you for the trials and snares,
Through it all, I knew how much you cared.
Thank you for that day on Calvary, and thank you for the day,
You set me free. but most of all Lord,
Thank you, Lord, for loving me.

He's the Son

He's the light on the darkest night,
And he's the reason I'm alive.
He's my will to survive,
He's the one, because He's the Son.
He's the one who died for me,
He's the one who set me free.
And he's the reason I believe,
He's the one,
Because he's the Son.

He's my strength every day,
He's the reason I won't stray.
He is why I'm on my way.
To that glory land someday.
He's the one, because he's the son.
He is the Son of God,
He's undying Love.
He is hope from above,
He's the one, because he's the son.

He's the Son up above,
He fills my whole life with love.
He's the one who leads the way,
He's in my heart every day.
He's the one, He's Gods Only Son.

Thankful

Well Jesus loved me so much,
That he gave up his life for me.
He never questioned,
Our Father in Heaven.
He knew his plan,
would soon set us free.

So, I Thank God who art in Heaven,
For that day, up on Calvary.
And I Thank Jesus for the suffering,
That he endured up there for me.

And I pray the Lord will forgive me,
For being so unworthy.
I want to thank Jesus,
For taking my place,
And I thank the Lord,
For he set me free.

Now Jesus awaits me in Heaven.
And I can't wait to see,
That Precious person,
Who gave his life for me.

Love Him

Love him with all your heart,
Every day.
Keep him in your heart,
In your work and in your play.

Because when you love from your heart,
You'll get love in return.
Love from the heart
 is a lesson you must learn.

Jesus gave his life for you,
Because he loved you so.
So, give him yours in return,

Hold on to him.
And don't let go.
The love he gives to you,
If you let it,
It will surely grow.

Love him with all your heart,
That's how it starts.
Give him all of it,
Not just a part.

I Want to See Jesus

I want to see Jesus,
 and the Apostle Paul.
I want to see Moses,
I want to see them all.

I want to hear the Angels,
Sing to me.
I want to see Jesus,
Because he died for me.

I want to see Noah, Peter, and John.
I want to see Andrew and Simeon.
When I reach Heaven,
There'll be so many to see.
So, I thank God,
For Heaven is eternity.

I want to see Mary,
Who gave us her son.
And then there's Abraham,
A friend to everyone.

I want to see Ruth and Naomi too,
And when I reach Heaven,
I want to see you.

I want to see Daniel,
And hear of the Lion's den.
I want to see Jonah and Joshua too.
I want to see Isaac and Rebekah too
 Thomas and Matthew, and Bartholomew.
But Lord when I reach Heaven,
Most of all I want to see you.

Why Won't They Believe?

Have you ever stopped to see?
The beauty of a tree.
It grows ever so tall.
With so many branches in the spring.
Beautiful green leaves,
Blowing in the wind.

In the fall leaves of many colors,
Paints a picture,
So beautiful and rare.
Each branch so different,
Some big and some small.

Yet they all come from the roots,
On the very same tree.
To some it's just a tree,
Made of bark, branches and leaves.

To me it is one of God's many blessings.
A vision of beauty for us to see.
Why won't they believe?
Have you ever seen the beauty?
Of the winters first snow.
Each snowflake different,
Yet together, they make a brilliant glow.

Why won't they believe?
And just think about the flowers
In the spring.
Bright, colorful, a sign of new life.
A new season for some,

A new beginning,
Of good things to come.
Why won't they believe?
Why is it so hard for some to believe?

In something so wonderful.
Who gave life to every living thing.
And the promise of everlasting life,
Our Father in Heaven.

I just can't imagine,
Why anyone wouldn't believe.
He makes it so easy to see the beauty,
In every living thing.
Why won't they believe?
After all we are just like the tree,
All so different.
But we came from the very same God,
So why not believe?

Can They See Jesus

Can they see Jesus when they look at you?

Do you represent Jesus in the things, you say and do?

Do you live like a Christian Every hour, every day?

before they'll want to be a Christian.

You must show them, what a Christian is like.

Then show them the way.

when they look at you, Will they see the likeness of Jesus?

Or the person you used to be.

Can they see it in your eyes?

Can they feel it from your heart?

Can they see the love?

That Jesus gave you, right from the very start.

Will you keep the fire burning?

The one you felt when you were saved.

Can you show them,

The wonderful blessing you receive.

When you hear, or speak his name,

if you ask yourself these questions,

What will your answer be?

I just hope that everyone I meet,

can see the Christian in me!

Rock for Ages

He's been my rock for ages,
 my shelter from the storm.
He gives me strength from up above.
 He protects me from all harm.
He is my strong foundation,
He is with me as I grow.
He's been my rock for ages.
 He's the only hope I know.

He's with me in the good times,
He's with me through the bad.
Of all the friends, I've known in life,
He's the best one that I've had.
He knows me better than I know myself,
 yet he forgives me of my wrongs.
He's been my rock for ages,
He's loved me all along.

Wherever life may lead me,

I'm sure that he will go.

Because when it comes to my future,

It's an answer only he could know.

If I'm in a valley, or on a mountain looking down.

He's the beauty that surrounds me,

 the only peace I've ever found.

We sailed through troubled waters,

 We've weathered every storm.

He's protected and guided me,

since the day that I was born.

He's been my rock for ages,

shelter in the storm.

Angel in Disguise

You must be an Angel in disguise.

From your warm friendly smile,

To your twinkling blue eyes.

Though I can't see a Halo,

A harp or wings that's true.

My description of an Angel,

Surely must be you.

For the land, you see around you,

You see through Gods eyes.

You are a friend to every man.

I'll remember you when I pray,

Because you bring sunshine,

To the darkest of days.

God whispered from Heaven,

And he told me it's true.

He sent me an Angel,

My friend it is you.

Keep on Walking

You better keep on walking,
 because the Devil is stalking you.
And don't you ever give up,
 because he is never through.

He might wear you down, but don't you fall.
Hold your head up high and stand up tall.
Shout up to Heaven, give the Lord a call.,
Keep on walking because the devil is stalking you.

He's around every corner, he's down every street.
But with the Lord's help, he can be beat.
So, keep on walking, because the Devil is stalking you.
He's the slyest fox that you'll ever meet.
He'll pour on the charm, and he'll seem so sweet.
He might be the stranger, that you chance to meet.
And given the chance, he'll knock you off your feet.
So, keep on walking, because the devil is stalking you.

The Father and the Son

When your life is weighing heavy on you,
 and there's nowhere left to turn.
Don't give up on hope,
 a life in Heaven you can earn.
If the pain in your heart,
 seems like more than you can bare.
Just hold on a little longer,
 for I know someone who cares.

Just reach up to Heaven,
and ask in the name of the Father,
And the Son. tell him that you're sorry,
And he'll forgive, all the things you've done.
Open your heart, and just let him in.
When you think, your life is over.
 This is where it begins.

Though sometimes it seems impossible,

Because of what you have done.

Remember everything is possible,

 through the power of,

The Father and the son.

 though you may not know it,

He knows every burden that you bare.

Just call upon him, and he'll show how much he cares.

In the name of the Father and the Son,

all bad things can be undone.

Though you're scared and felling lonely,

Don't hide your face and run.

If somethings tugging at your heart,

It's probably the Father and the Son.

There was a day up on Calvary,

just before the setting sun.

Jesus said Father forgive them,

for they know not what they have done.

Every soul can have redemption,

because of the Mercy of Our Father,

And the blood of his son.

I'll Be Satisfied

Here on earth, it seems,
 People are always searching.
For something that they need,
 to make them whole.
Searching never to find the answer,
 In this troubled land,
We live in here below.

 If they would just ask,
They too could find the answer.
what makes me happy in this world,
We're in today.
 I once like them,
 was searching for the answer.
For peace and joy within.
until one day when I had a talk with him.

You see I laid my troubles,

 down at the Altar,

When I went to the Lord in Prayer.

 He forgave me of my sins.

Now I'm waiting for the day,

 I'll get to Heaven.

Eternally I'll have Peace and Joy within.

 until then I'll keep waiting and watching,

And I'll be satisfied,

when I'm up there with him.

Jesus Hold My Hand

Precious Jesus hold my hand,

Walk with me through this troubled land.

If I should stumble, please understand,

I need you Jesus to hold my hand.

Guide me gently from day to day.

Help me Jesus as I travel on.

This world is full of sorrow and pain,

I have so little to lose and so much to gain.

So, if I stumble, please understand,

I need you Jesus to hold my hand,

Walk with me daily hand in hand,

Lead me to the promised land.

Precious Jesus hold my hand.

I Believe

I believe the sun shines,
 to dry the morning dew.
And I believe there is a Heaven,
somewhere beyond the blue.
I believe in miracles,
 because I have found one in you.

I believe God gave me the best of miracles,
When he gave me a friend like you.
someone who doesn't judge me,
For all the things I do.

 someone who can forgive me,
For all the wrongs, I make.
 and Lord knows I've made a few.
Someone who makes me feel beautiful,
On my ugliest of days.
someone who never downs me,

But lifts me up with praise.
someone who always thinks of me,
In thoughtful and caring ways.

Someone always willing to listen,
 whenever I need an ear.
Someone with whom I 've shared,
 my deepest secrets and fears.
Someone who has been there,
to wipe away my tears.
You are my special friend,
 and you will be throughout the years.

I believe in miracles, and I believe in you.
 I believe there is a tenderness,
In everything you do.
 I believe you are special,
In your very own way

my friend you are the sunshine,

On my darkest of days.

you have a gift about you,

That few have taken the time to see.

but I'm so glad you've taken the time,

To share your gift with me.

you give me hope,

When I feel, there is none in sight.

when my day is gloomy,

You make everything so bright,

thank you, my friend,

For being a very special part of my life.

There are little things about you,

That I've taken the time to see.

like the different ways that you smile,

I know there's at least three. my favorite one,

Is when you're smiling at me.

No matter what anyone ever thinks about you,

you will always be

a very special blessing to me. this I know, This I believe!

Your Little Boy's Hero

Your little boy is special, he's one of a kind.

From his cute little dimples to his big blue eyes.

You work such long hours, but he doesn't really seem to mind.

When you come home from the road, you'll see the joy that he can't hide.

Your little boy has a hero, and he's my hero too.

We both love our hero, and our hero is you.

I can tell he loves you, and I know you love him too.

But in case you don't know, your little boy's hero,

Is my hero too.

 Everyone has a hero,

To most they're one of a kind.

but no one has a hero,

Like your little boy's and mine.

your little boy has a hero,

he's my hero too. we both love our hero,

And our hero is you.

40 Years

They say it all started,

 with a man and his dream.

But who could have known?

 He would go this extreme.

He started with family,

and a few chosen friends.

Trying to make a living,

and tie up loose ends.

Employees have come,

 employees have gone.

As we look back,

 We sometimes wonder.

How their time is now spent.

 it was just a little store on Choctaw Street,

As time went on, he built #2.

And as the years passed,

 his company grew.

Expanding to Tulsa, Owasso and Jenks.

Sapulpa and Langley, and 41st street.

Through good times and bad times,

 his company endured.

The man knows his business,

That's for sure.

It's been a lot of hard work,

 sweat and sometimes tears.

But together we look forward,

to our next forty years.

All Around Cowboy

No one knows where he came from,

No one knew where he'd been.

He was a good - looking cowboy,

with a George Strait type of grin.

He wore a Stetson hat, wrangler jeans.

and Tony Lama boots.

There isn't a calf that he can't rope,

there isn't a bull that he can't ride.

He can bust those broncs,

He has a grace within.

Cause out of all he has,

The thing I like most is his style.

He can hold 1st place, six nights in a row.

If you let him, he can steal the show.

He's stolen ladies' hearts,

for miles, around.

So, you'd better beware,

 if he rides through your town.

Hey all - around cowboy, come show me around.

He's an all- around cowboy,

who can turn your world around.

A Letter from Dad

I'm looking through,
  old memories of yesterday.
Some of them I'll keep,
  and some I'll throw away.
Some of them make me speechless,
  I don't know what to say.

There are a few pictures,
of friends that I've had.
But what I noticed most,
  Is just one letter from my dad.

In dad's letter, he said, "I love you."
It might have meant something,
  if he'd shown me that he cared.
But what I looked for in the letter,
  just wasn't there.

I wanted him to say, "I'm proud of you."

But that was always something,

Dad would never do.

It hurts me sometimes,

 because things are the way they are.

And at times I still hope,

 someday he'll be proud,

Of just one thing that I do.

But if he ever is,

He'd never admit it's true.

Just one letter is all that I have,

 From a man,

Who calls himself my dad.

Why Did He Have to Go?

There's a reason for everything,
that goes on in our lives.
There's hatred and love,
 weakness and strife.
But tell me what the reason is,
 that one man should take a life?

I want to know the reason,
 So please just tell me why.
Why did he have to go?

Tell me the reason why,
 I really want to know,
Why does a young man die?

If there really is a reason,
 Now is when I want to know.
There's so much pain and sorrow,

So why did he have to go?

We all understand,

that we will die someday.

But why did he have to go,

In such a cruel hearted way?

We also understand.

that the innocent usually die,

While the guilty run away.

Surely, we all know.

That God will deal with the guilty in time.

But will he feel the pain we felt,

the night that young man died.

Nothing will replace his life,

 and all we have left is the memories,

Of good times that we shared.

 another thing we must realize,

Does the guilty man know?

Just how much, and why we really cared?

Why did he have to go?

Tell me the reason why.

 I really want to know,

Why does a young man die?

If there really is a reason,

now is when I want to know.

There's so much pain and sorrow,

So why did he have to go.

Daddy Don't Shout

Why is it so hard for adults to forgive?

So, they'll keep loving each other,

 and learn to forget.

It doesn't take much for a child to get mad.

Like when they are scolded,

Or sent early to bed.

But our little girl loves us,

And she never stays mad.

So, I just couldn't imagine why this morning she said.

Early last night when you put me to bed,

I listened to what both of you said.

Daddy don't shout,

 and make mommy sad.

Mommy don't cry,

when daddy gets mad.

I know that he loves you,

and you love him too.

But how can she trust you,

when you won't tell the truth.

But if you keep fighting,

 Your love will soon end.

When you stop fighting,

you soon start over again.

Daddy don't shout,

and make mommy sad.

Mommy don't cry when daddy gets mad.

If you can't love each other,

Then how can you love me?

If you'd just stop and listen,

then maybe you'd see.

When you hurt each other,

You hurt me too.

And when your mad at each other,

It makes me mad at you.

So, Daddy don't shout,

and make mommy sad.

And mommy don't cry,

when daddy gets mad.

Because when you're hurting each other,

You're hurting me too.

Good Intentions

A lot of folks have good intentions,

They have them every day.

But don't let your good intentions,

Lead you astray.

Do what you must and do it today.

There may not be tomorrow,

When you could have done it yesterday.

United We Stand

United we stand, but divided we fall.

We should love one another after it all.

We all came from one man, that's how it began.

But what's happening now, is getting out of hand.

We started out as friends; swore we'd be until the end.

But something went terribly wrong.

Fathers, Mothers, Sisters and Brothers,

Slowly growing apart.

Why can't they stay friends?

And remain that way until the end.

It's breaking their hearts in two.

He made the skies, and the stars up above.

He made our hearts so that we could love.

He made the trees,

And the flowers that bloom.

He made me, and he made you.

I don't believe hatred was in his plan,

He wants you to love your fellow man.

It's time to forgive the person,

Even though they have sinned.

We can all live in peace,

If we try, I know we can.

Grandpa

When I was just a little girl,

I sat upon your knee.

A frail old man with a gentle smile,

As sweet as you could be.

A special person is what you were,

Though simple as can be.

I didn't get to know you long,

But you meant the world to me.

All I have is a memory,

Of a man who loved me so.

I miss you dearly,

But I know, you thought the world of me.

You taught me to love Jesus,

So that one day I could see.

You are sitting up there in heaven with Jesus,

Watching over me.

Remember

Remember when he died for you,

And remember when he pulled you through.

Remember when his blood was shed,

And how he rose, when some thought he was dead.

When you are down and feeling blue,

Just remember when he died for you.

When it seems like there is no hope in sight,

Just ask the Lord, and he will make everything alright.

Through a Child's Eyes

Have you ever stopped to see this World,

the way it was meant to be seen.

The way a child see's it and treasures everything.

We think of them as innocent,

And needing to learn so much.

But if you stop and listen,

You will see who is out of touch.

Have you ever stopped to see the world through a child's eyes?

If you could see the world the way they see it,

I think you would be surprised.

I'm sure you did not long ago,

But it's a moment that's lost in time.

A child see's things so differently,

They see the world the way it was meant to be seen.

You see a rock, and to you it's just a stone,

But to them it's a treasure,

God has sent to them from his Throne.

Have you ever looked up in the sky,

 to see the clouds above?

When you look at them,

What do you see?

They might see a butterfly,

or maybe an angel is what they see.

Whatever it is,

 they know it is a beautiful gift from God to you and me.

Have you thought about the stars

 that he hung up in the sky?

We look at them and do not see the gift

 He gave to light the darkest night.

Some things they do,

we might think are silly,

But if you looked at things the way they do.

You just might see they are wiser than any man.

You would see the things we take for granted, every day.

You would see they are treasures,

God has given us upon this land.

If you are searching for happiness

and peace that is deep within,

Try to see the world through the eyes of a child,

And you will find peace again.

Above and Beyond

I've risen above your expectations of me,

And I've went beyond what I thought I could be.

Now you would be surprised in the changes in me.

Thanks for not believing in me.

Because of you I am successful

And I owe it all to you.

There was a time I must admit it's true,

I didn't believe in myself because of you.

But I have risen above your expectations of me,

And I have gone beyond what I thought I could be.

You said I could never make it out there on my own,

But I am living proof life does go on.

I took the chance to believe in myself, when,

 No one else would.

I took the chance and did the best that I could.

Because of you I went above what you thought I could be.

And I went beyond your expectations of me.

The Creature

Who was the creature from the Black Lagoon?

Filled with vengeance,

 hatred and gloom.

Who was the monster who caused me such fear?

Who scared me to death,

any time he came near.

Who could have loved him,

 and kept him around?

Never a smile and always a frown.

The beatings and torture,

 the hurt and the pain,

Determined to slowly make me go insane.

The haunting old memories,

are always the same.

Who could it be,

 What is his name?

Dad, though I am sure he and Satan

 are one and the same.

When My Life Is Through

I wonder what they will say,

when my life is through.

I wonder if they will miss me,

 will they be lonesome and blue?

Will I leave them fond memories,

to carry them through?

I wonder what they will say,

when my life is through.

Will they count up the good deeds that I have done?

Or will they search really hard and not even find one.

Will they sing and rejoice and be glad that I am gone,

Or will they be broken hearted,

 because they have lost their loved one?

I wonder what they will do when my life is through.

Will they hang their head in sorrow,

and be lonesome and blue?

Will they grieve for a long time,
 or just a week or two?
I wonder what they will do,
 when my life is through.

I just hope they will remember,
 when my life is through.
How much I love them,
and how I will miss them too.

I hope they will go on,
and find happiness again.
I hope they won't mourn long,
 Life is too short to be bleak and dim.

I wish them a life,

full of love and good friends.

And I will be waiting in Heaven until I see them again.

But until then,

I wonder what they will say when my life is through.

P.O.W

He was a Soldier,
 when he was a young man.
He was left in a rice field,
 in a place called Vietnam.

What started out as a conflict,
 suddenly got way out of hand.
The things that he saw,
 shouldn't be described by any fellow man.

Feeling all alone, confused by a War,
 that he didn't understand.
Some people were for it,
 and some just didn't care.
But all he knew was,
 he just wanted out of there.

Late one night,

  his biggest fear came to light.

He was captured by the enemy,

  while fighting for his life.

He suddenly became a prisoner of War.

Suffering tortures,

he had never known before.

Not knowing where he was,

  or if he would survive.

By the Grace of God,

They kept him alive.

For seven long years,

  he remained in that World,

Praying daily to God,

  but still unsure.

The War finally ended,

and he was set free.

But time wouldn't heal

 the damage inside you see.

He still remains a prisoner inside of his head,

Haunted and tortured until he is dead.

The memories stay with him, like demons within.

Nothing can tame them,

They will be with him until the very end.

He is still a prisoner inside his weary soul,

and he will remain one until he is cold.

A Soldiers Journey

I am a Soldier for the red, white and blue,

I'm willing to give my life for many people that's true.

Sometimes it's a struggle in this life that I decided to choose.

But before you judge me,

 walk a mile in my shoes.

The pain and the torture,

My friend, may you never know.

But I am a soldier so I can't let it show.

I entered the service, fresh out of school.

Thinking this life would be kind of cool.

I would travel to many distant lands,

Helping one another, lending a helping hand.

Soon after my basics, I received the call.

And I began the journey that would change it all.

I flew into the battlefield in a foreign distant land,

Not knowing what would happen,

Not knowing God's plan.

Away from my family, my home and my friends.

My machine gun beside me,

became my very best friend.

Imminent danger was right ahead.

There were so many wounded,

and many more were dead.

Facing a fear no one can describe,

The gut-wrenching memories torture me inside.

Time has passed and the war has come to an end.

But the battle is not over,

I keep reliving it again and again.

The flashes and visions take me back there each day,

Will it ever be over,

before I go insane?

I've seen so many doctors I can't even begin to recall.

Repeating my symptoms and reliving it all.

Reliving the nightmare,

such torture and pain,

Surely, I think I must be going insane.

What is the matter, what is wrong with me?

The doctors all call it P.T.S.D.

But if you ask me,

it's sad but it's true,

It's Hell on earth until my life is through.

It's time now soldier,

 to put down your gun.

Your battle is finished and peace you have finally won.

My time on earth may be over, but my life has just begun.

I know it was worth it,

all that I went through,

I am in God's army now,

and I am watching over you.

Be Still My Heart

Be still my heart, Calm my fears.

Guide me through, my golden years.

Build me up with courage and strength.

Show me which path that I should take.

Be there to catch me if I should fall.

Be my comfort through it all.

Stairway to Heaven

Let me tell you a story my grandpa told once to me,

When I was only a baby at the tender age of three.

He said child there's a stairway to Heaven,

that you will want to climb,

like grandma and me when it's our time.

There is treasures and riches unending,

there is beauty and angels all around,

just keep climbing that stairway one step at a time.

Reach out to Jesus and glory you will find.

Don't listen to Satan, he will lead you astray.

Keep pushing him farther away when you pray.

Give your heart to Jesus,

your mind, your body and soul.

Give your whole heart to Jesus,

So that one day you can walk on the streets of gold.

A mansion is waiting for you to call home.

Hold on to Jesus,

and you will never be alone.

He will carry your burdens,

and calm your fears.

He will be right beside you,

throughout your years.

Window in Heaven

There's a window In Heaven,
 so that they can see.
I know he is up there,
 waiting patiently for me.

There's a doorway in Heaven,
 It's opened wide.
It's waiting for me to step on inside.

There's a mansion in Heaven,
 for me to call home.
There are Angels in Heaven,
 singing so sweet.
Hopefully they will sing one day for me.
There's a stairway to Heaven that I long to climb.
I want to go to Heaven whenever it's my time.

Made in the USA
Middletown, DE
10 November 2024